LIFE WORKS ITSELF OUT

· · · · · · ·

(AND THEN YOU NAP)

Keiya Mizuno & Naoki Naganuma

TOUCHSTONE

New York   London   Toronto   Sydney   New Delhi

Touchstone
An Imprint of Simon & Schuster, Inc.
1230 Avenue of the Americas
New York, NY 10020

First Touchstone trade paperback edition October 2016

TOUCHSTONE and colophon are registered trademarks of
Simon & Schuster, Inc.

For information about special discounts for bulk purchases, please contact Simon & Schuster Special Sales at 1-866-506-1949 or business@simonandschuster.com.

The Simon & Schuster Speakers Bureau can bring authors to your live event. For more information or to book an event, contact the Simon & Schuster Speakers Bureau at 1-866-248-3049 or visit our website at www.simonspeakers.com.

Interior design by Jill Putorti
Book design of the original edition: Bunpei Yorifuji, Ayaka Kitatani, and Kentaro Sugiyama
Key advisor: Taku Tsuboi

Manufactured in the United States of America

10 9 8 7 6 5 4 3 2 1

Library of Congress Cataloging-in-Publication Data

Names: Mizuno, Keiya, author. | Naganuma, Naoki, author.
Title: Life works itself out : and then you nap / Mizuno
    Keiya & Naganuma Naoki.
Other titles: Jinsei wa nyantoka naru! English
Description: New York : Touchstone, [2016] | Includes bibliographical
    references.
Identifiers: LCCN 2016024583 (print) | LCCN 2016038042 (ebook) | ISBN
    9781501127854 (paperback) | ISBN 9781501127861 (Ebook)
Subjects: LCSH: Cats—Humor. | Cats—Pictorial works. | Conduct of
    life—Humor. | BISAC: HUMOR / Form / Anecdotes. | PETS / Cats /
    General. | HUMOR / Topic / Animals.
Classification: LCC PN6231.C23 M59 2016 (print) | LCC PN6231.C23 (ebook) |
    DDC 818/.602—dc23
LC record available at https://lccn.loc.gov/2016024583

ISBN 978-1-5011-2785-4
ISBN 978-1-5011-2786-1 (ebook)

If you ever lose your way,
the best thing to do is to follow a cat.
Cats never lose their way.

CHARLES M. SCHULZ

CONTENTS

The sixty-eight cats are separated into seven categories, each grouped by their "Words of Wisdom." The top of each page is numbered so that you can enjoy reading the book in any order. Some readers may prefer to begin reading the first part, "Start," while others may want to proceed with their favorite categories in any order.

LIFE WORKS
ITSELF OUT

· · · · · · · · ·

START

· 1 ·

A LITTLE CLUMSINESS CAN BE CHARMING.

Marilyn Monroe, American actress (1926–1962)

Marilyn Monroe, with her signature red lipstick and beauty mark, made quite an impression in the 1953 hit film *Niagara*. It was in this film that the so-called Monroe walk first appeared, in which Marilyn famously sashayed across the screen with her hips swaying drastically from side to side. This was, in fact, Marilyn's own idea. She purposely unbalanced herself by making the heel of her right shoe about a quarter inch shorter than that of the left, forcing her to use her hips and waist in order to keep her balance.

People aren't necessarily seeking perfection. Sometimes our faults and shortcomings make us more attractive.

QUOTES OF THE GREATS

"There are some people who only disgust with their abilities; and there are some people who please even with their faults."
—FRANÇOIS DE LA ROCHEFOUCAULD, FRENCH ARISTOCRAT (1613–1680)

"There are defects so bound to fine qualities that they announce them, defects which it is well not to correct."
—JOSEPH JOUBERT, FRENCH PHILOSOPHER (1754–1824)

"Clear water cannot harbor big fish."
—BAN CHAO, CHINESE GENERAL (32–102 **AD**)

GET COMPLETELY INTO IT.

Coco Chanel, French fashion designer (1883–1971)

When perfume was first invented, the raw ingredients were flowers. But perfume made from flowers would, after some time, lose its aroma, and the particular flowers whose fragrances the perfume contained could easily be identified. Chanel was the one who started the perfume revolution. She dreamed of making a perfume whose mysterious aroma makes a woman's heart race—whose scent does not fade, and whose ingredients cannot easily be determined. So she worked with fragrance chemists, shut away in her laboratory, testing countless formulas, trying out different ingredients, getting closer and closer to the scent she had been dreaming of. She continued in this process until, finally, with its secret formula of over eighty ingredients, Chanel Nº5 was born.

If we pursue our dreams and ambitions, we can bring new and wonderful things into the world.

"Nothing great was ever achieved without enthusiasm."
—RALPH WALDO EMERSON, AMERICAN ESSAYIST (1803–1882)

"Be intensely in earnest. Enthusiasm invites enthusiasm."
—RUSSELL CONWELL, AMERICAN MINISTER (1843–1925)

"The man or woman of enthusiastic trend always exercises a magnetic influence over those with whom he or she comes in contact."
—H. ADDINGTON BRUCE, AMERICAN AUTHOR (1874–1959)

LAUGH AT LEAST ONCE A DAY.

Thomas Edison, American industrialist and inventor (1847–1931)

There may not be another person who took laughing as seriously as Thomas Edison. Even when he had lost most of his hearing, he would laugh and say that it made it easier for him to concentrate on his experiments and research. One night, as he watched a fire consume his factory, he was so fascinated by the beautiful scene of the fire that he called his father on the telephone so he could describe the beauty to him. What's even more remarkable is that after witnessing the fire that night, Edison realized that the smoke obscured the firefighters' fields of vision, making it impossible to fight the fire. So he quickly invented a high-powered searchlight for firefighters to use. You might say that Edison's inventions were born from the idea that no matter how difficult life got, he never forgot to laugh.

Sometimes things happen in our day-to-day lives that we are not happy about. But in these times especially, the one thing we cannot forget to do is laugh.

QUOTES OF THE GREATS

"The most wasted of all days is one without laughter."
—NICOLAS CHAMFORT, FRENCH THINKER (1741–1794)

"Life without laughing is a dreary blank."
—WILLIAM MAKEPEACE THACKERAY, ENGLISH NOVELIST (1811–1863)

"Perhaps I know best why it is man alone who laughs; he alone suffers so deeply that he had to invent laughter."
—FRIEDRICH NIETZSCHE, GERMAN PHILOSOPHER (1844–1900)

THE OPPORTUNITY WON'T COME UNLESS YOU ASK FOR IT.

Mariah Carey, American singer (1970–)

World-famous singer-songwriter Mariah Carey had a legendary opportunity. Before her rise to fame, she would always carry around a demo tape when she went out. At a chance meeting at a party, she got a copy of her tape to Sony Music chairman Tommy Mottola. He listened to the demo in his car on the way home, but then rushed back to the party to sign Mariah to a record contract.

Even if you have a voice like Mariah Carey's, you can't just wait for something to happen; you have to be constantly searching for your chance. Always play to your abilities and seize any opportunity.

"Trust thyself: every heart vibrates to that iron string."
—RALPH WALDO EMERSON, AMERICAN ESSAYIST (1803–1882)

"What's the good of living if you don't try a few things?"
—CHARLES M. SCHULZ, AMERICAN CARTOONIST (1922–2000)

"You have to free your mind to do things you wouldn't think of doing. Don't ever say no."
—CARL LEWIS, AMERICAN TRACK AND FIELD ATHLETE (1961–)

QUOTES OF THE GREATS

DOESN'T YOUR FACE SAY IT ALL?

Katsu Kaishū, Japanese naval officer and statesman (1823–1899)

This story began when Katsu Kaishū entered a local eatery called The Green Willow. As Katsu looked around the inside of the establishment, he saw the proprietor busily cleaning tables and serving customers rice cakes. Katsu said to the proprietor, "Business looks good." "Not at all," she replied. "We don't have a cent to spare. My husband is out right now looking for other ways to raise money. But I know the secret to staying popular and in business, and it isn't easy. You can't let your customers or employees see you struggle." In that moment, Katsu understood that that was also the secret to diplomacy, and to everything else in life. Katsu thanked the proprietor, saying, "I have learned very much from our encounter," and, as the story goes, he offered the proprietor the thirty *ryō* he had on hand, the equivalent of around $10,000.

Even when things get tough, don't complain; keep your head up and look well. That's the secret to bringing happiness into your life.

QUOTES OF THE GREATS

"Often a silent face has voice and words."
—OVID, ROMAN POET (43 BC–17 AD)

"There are mystically in our faces certain characters which carry in them the motto of our souls, wherein he that cannot read A, B, C may read our natures."
—THOMAS BROWNE, ENGLISH AUTHOR AND DOCTOR (1605–1682)

"Showing a fresh and cheerful expression is the foundation of human morality."
—YUKICHI FUKUZAWA, JAPANESE AUTHOR AND ENTREPRENEUR (1835–1901)

A SHARED DREAM MEANS EVEN MORE.

Hanaoka Seishū, Edo period physician (1760–1835)

Hanaoka Seishū is credited with successfully producing the world's first general anesthetic, but he did not succeed on his own. Hanaoka's mother, Otsugi, and wife, Kae, volunteered as test subjects to determine the effects of the anesthetics, and Kae lost her eyesight as a result. What's more, it is said that ten people, starting with Hanaoka's relatives, offered themselves toward the development of the drugs. This led to the successful development of the general anesthetic by Hanaoka, who was able to perform surgery on 143 infants and saved many lives.

The dreams that we share with many lead to the greatest achievements, not the dreams we keep to ourselves.

"A dream you dream alone is only a dream. A dream you dream together is reality."
—JOHN LENNON, BRITISH SINGER AND SONGWRITER (1940–1980)

"Talent wins games, but teamwork and intelligence wins championships."
—MICHAEL JORDAN, AMERICAN BASKETBALL PLAYER (1963–)

"You are lost if you forget that the fruits of the earth belong to all and the earth to no one!"
—JEAN-JACQUES ROUSSEAU, FRENCH THINKER (1712–1778)

SLACK OFF EVEN ONCE
AND IT BECOMES A HABIT.

Mencius, Confucian philosopher (372–289 BC)

The great Confucian philosopher Mencius, who advocated that human nature is fundamentally good, was raised by a mother who had a passion for her son's education. On one particular day when he did not want to study, young Mencius returned home and was asked by his mother how far along he had progressed in his studies. Mencius answered apologetically, "The same as before." On hearing this, his mother stopped her work at the loom, took out a knife, and slashed the textile she had been weaving to shreds. Shocked, Mencius asked his mother why she had done this, to which she replied, "Quitting your studies before you have finished is the same thing as me cutting up my unfinished cloth like this." Mencius reflected on his mother's words, and from then on he worked on his studies from morning till night.

When you neglect your work, you may lose the will to continue. Face your daily challenges with enthusiasm and passion.

"Iron rusts from disuse; stagnant water loses its purity and in cold weather becomes frozen; even so does inaction sap the vigor of the mind."

—LEONARDO DA VINCI, ITALIAN ARTIST AND INVENTOR (1452–1519)

"Laziness may appear attractive, but work gives satisfaction."

—ANNE FRANK, AUTHOR OF *THE DIARY OF A YOUNG GIRL* (1929–1945)

"By the streets of 'By and By,' one arrives at the house of 'Never.'"

—MIGUEL DE CERVANTES, SPANISH AUTHOR (1547–1616)

QUOTES OF THE GREATS

IN PLACES UNSEEN, A HERO IS THERE.

Douglas C. Prasher, American molecular biologist (1951–)

In the late 1980s, Douglas Prasher carried out research on the green fluorescent protein found in jellyfish under a grant from the American Cancer Society. Three years later, after successfully reproducing the green fluorescent protein, Prasher shared his discoveries with other researchers, including the renowned scientist Martin Chalfie. Prasher intended to continue his research on green fluorescent protein, but after failing to receive further funding, he was forced to leave his job. In October 2008, when Martin Chalfie, Osamu Shimomura, and Roger Tsien received the Nobel Prize for their work on green fluorescent protein, Prasher's name was not among the recipients. At that time, Prasher, who was working as a shuttle driver for a car dealership, said, "I personally believe you have an obligation to share. I put my heart and soul into it, but if I kept that stuff, it wasn't gonna go anyplace."

The world is held up by unsung heroes like Prasher, who we find in even the darkest places.

QUOTES OF THE GREATS

"Nothing truly valuable arises from ambition or from a mere sense of duty; it stems rather from love and devotion towards men and towards objective things."
—ALBERT EINSTEIN, GERMAN PHYSICIST (1879–1955)

"Do not despair at being an unsung hero. Always keep in your heart the desire to do what is right for mankind."
—MAEJIMA HISOKA, JAPANESE STATESMAN AND POLITICIAN (1835–1919)

"Be still, sad heart! and cease repining;
Behind the clouds is the sun still shining."
—HENRY WADSWORTH LONGFELLOW, AMERICAN POET (1807–1882)

WORK
· · · · · · · · · · · ·

OPPORTUNITY IN A SMALL SPACE.

Masaru Ibuka, cofounder of Sony (1908–1997)

In 1946, not long after World War II ended, Ibuka Masaru gave the following speech to his twenty employees at the founding ceremony of Tokyo Telecommunications Engineering Corporation, the original name of Sony. "If we try to do what the big companies do, we will surely fail. But there are many gaps in the current technology. We will do what the big companies cannot do and use our new technology to help rebuild our country." And just as he said, Sony developed unparalleled technology and enjoyed rapid success. Ibuka is also credited with coming up with the idea for Sony's hit product the Walkman while he was president of Sony. Even though most of the people at Sony opposed the idea of selling a tape player that did not have recording capabilities, Ibuka was the first to see the niche opportunity, and set the product into development.

There are untapped opportunities in every field. That is where the treasure lies.

QUOTES OF THE GREATS

"The beginnings of all things are small."
—CICERO, ROMAN STATESMAN (106–43 BC)

"Creative and original ideas start out in the minority. Things of the majority are not original."
—HIDEKI YUKAWA, JAPANESE PHYSICIST (1907–1981)

(When asked about the competition that he feared the most)
"The two guys inventing away in a garage somewhere."
—BILL GATES, COFOUNDER OF MICROSOFT (1955–)

MAKE IT A HABIT TO SAY "I'LL TAKE CARE OF IT."

Kevin Costner, American actor (1955–)

Singer Whitney Houston was unsure when she first got offered the part in the movie *The Bodyguard*. She didn't have any experience on a movie set, and if the film were to be a failure, her fans would be very disappointed. She agonized over whether or not to accept the offer for two years, but the one who was by her side encouraging her was Kevin Costner, the man who would play her bodyguard in the film. "I promised her two things," he says. "That I would be right there with her, and she would not be bad, because I refuse to let anybody fail around me." With Kevin's encouragement, Whitney accepted the offer, and *The Bodyguard* became a huge success.

People follow the person who can say with confidence, "I'll take care of it."

QUOTES OF THE GREATS

"The price of greatness is responsibility."

—WINSTON CHURCHILL, BRITISH STATESMAN AND AUTHOR (1874–1965)

"The best way to assert one's authority is to solve the problems that trouble his subordinates."

—HONORÉ DE BALZAC, FRENCH AUTHOR (1799–1850)

"A leader is a dealer in hope."

—NAPOLEON BONAPARTE, FRENCH EMPEROR AND MILITARY LEADER (1769–1821)

DON'T LOOK AWAY FROM REALITY.

Andrew Grove, American businessman (1936–2016)

In the 1970s, semiconductor maker Intel had a monopoly on the memory chip industry, but competitors quickly began to enter the market. By the early 1980s, Japanese companies were already developing memory chips that were of higher quality than Intel's and quickly swept the market. At that time, Andrew Grove spoke with Intel's cofounder Gordon Moore, and asked him, "If we got kicked out and the board brought in a new CEO, what do you think he would do?" Gordon immediately replied, "He would get us out of memories." Then Grove said, "Why shouldn't you and I walk out the door, come back in, and do it ourselves?" And just like that, Intel really did get out of the memory chip business, focused on microprocessors, and breathed new life into the company.

Taking a hard, objective look at reality does not come without pain. But that's how we are able to see what should be done.

"Strength is seeing yourself as you are."
—TARŌ OKAMOTO, JAPANESE ARTIST (1911–1996)

"Acceptance of what has happened is the first step to overcoming the consequences of any misfortune."
—WILLIAM JAMES, AMERICAN PSYCHOLOGIST (1842–1910)

QUOTES OF THE GREATS

I'M ALL EARS.

Higuchi Hirotaro, honorary president of Asahi Breweries (1926–2012)
Higuchi Hirotaro became president of Asahi Breweries, meaning "Rising Sun" Breweries, when the company held a perpetually low share of the beer market. Other brewers often ridiculed Asahi as Yuhi ("Setting Sun") Breweries. But Higuchi was determined to discover the reason for the company's poor performance, so he directly sought the advice of his rivals at Kirin Brewery and Sapporo Breweries. Bowing his head, he implored, "Tell me what we are doing wrong." Higuchi valued criticism most of all, and would go around soliciting complaints and requests from alcohol vendors. Because of Higuchi's commitment to carefully listening to others' opinions, Asahi was able to produce Super Dry and other hit beers and strengthened their place in the industry.

Higuchi said that his willingness to admit that he "was a novice in the beer industry" was what allowed him to innovate. Success comes to those who listen to what others have to say without getting stuck in their own thoughts.

QUOTES OF THE GREATS

"We have two ears and one mouth, so we should listen more than we talk."
—ZENO OF CITIUM, GREEK PHILOSOPHER (334–262 BC)

"Your most unhappy customers are your greatest source of learning."
—BILL GATES, COFOUNDER OF MICROSOFT (1955–)

"The wise listen, but fools speak."
—SOLOMON, KING OF ISRAEL (990–931 BC)

Anton Chekhov, Russian playwright (1860–1904)

At age nineteen, Anton Chekhov, the Russian playwright who would become known for his masterpiece *The Seagull* and other plays, was studying to become a doctor. His financial situation was desperate, so he began submitting short stories to a popular magazine. Chekhov saved the money he made from his stories, which were light and easy to read, and he continued his side job after becoming a doctor. But upon receiving an admiring letter from the celebrated Russian author Dmitry Grigorovich that said, "You have *real* talent—a talent which places you in the front rank among writers in the new generation," Chekhov began to approach his writing in earnest, slowing down to create better-quality work and focusing his energies solely on writing.

A big chance might come along when you're least expecting it, so grab on when it does.

"A wise man will make more opportunities than he finds."
—FRANCIS BACON, ENGLISH PHILOSOPHER (1561–1626)

"Action may not always bring happiness; but there is no happiness without action."
—BENJAMIN DISRAELI, BRITISH POLITICIAN (1804–1881)

"The man who insists upon seeing with perfect clearness before he decides, never decides."
—HENRI-FRÉDÉRIC AMIEL, SWISS POET (1821–1881)

NO EMBARRASSMENT IN DEPENDING ON OTHERS.

Karl Marx, German philosopher and economist (1818–1883)

While Karl Marx was in London writing *Capital, Volume 1*, his friend and collaborator Friedrich Engels was working in Manchester in order to help Marx and his several children with their living expenses. After Marx finished writing *Capital, Volume 1*, Engels sent Marx a letter saying, "I have some cheques here so that if you are short of cash, do not feel embarrassed but let me know how much you need." Marx did not feel indebted, but instead repaid Engels by devoting all his energy to his work. Marx unfortunately died before *Capital* was completed, but Engels fulfilled Marx's dying wish and edited the second and third volumes of *Capital* based on the latter's transcripts.

Do your best in the things you can do, and depend on the strengths of others for the things you cannot do. This way you will end up with the greatest benefit for everyone.

QUOTES OF THE GREATS

"**It marks a big step in your development when you come to realize that other people can help you do a better job than you could do alone.**"

—ANDREW CARNEGIE, AMERICAN INDUSTRIALIST (1835–1919)

"**I not only use all the brains that I have, but all that I can borrow.**"

—WOODROW WILSON, TWENTY-EIGHTH PRESIDENT OF THE UNITED STATES (1856–1924)

Jeff Bezos, founder of Amazon (1964–)

Jeff Bezos founded the online retailer Amazon in 1994. At the start, when all orders were placed via e-mail, Amazon had only four employees and one computer, and Bezos handled the delivery packaging himself. As he did this work, Bezos realized that in order for online shopping to become more popular, there needed to be a way to make a purchase in one click. So, in 1999, Amazon acquired the 1-Click patent. Today the technology has become commonplace, but for Amazon, acquiring the patent at a time before the Internet's ubiquity allowed the company to rise to the top of online retail. The patent is still in effect today, and even Apple's iTunes Store makes use of the technology.

When you're the first to do something, you can steer its development to your advantage.

QUOTES OF THE GREATS

"First come, first served."
—SIMA QIAN, CHINESE HISTORIAN (C. 145–C. 87 BC)

"Speed will be the most important thing for businesses."
—BILL GATES, COFOUNDER OF MICROSOFT (1955–)

"The first blow is half the battle."
—OLIVER GOLDSMITH, ENGLISH PLAYWRIGHT (1730–1774)

DON'T FEAR CONFLICT.

Steve Jobs, cofounder of Apple (1955–2011)

Apple's cofounder Steve Jobs was not afraid of conflict. One time, he demanded that the boot time be reduced for the Macintosh computers under development, and he did not back down when the engineer expressed disapproval. "If it would save a person's life, would you find a way to shave ten seconds off the boot time?" Jobs asked. He continued, explaining that if five million potential Mac users wasted an extra ten seconds each day booting up, that would come to around 300 million hours per year. In other words, the time saved would be equivalent to at least one hundred lifetimes a year. His words resonated with the engineer, who worked over the next couple of weeks and was able to reduce the boot time by twenty-eight seconds.

Don't be afraid to challenge opinions in order to create something better.

QUOTES OF THE GREATS

"Honest disagreement is often a good sign of progress."
—MAHATMA GANDHI, INDIAN LAWYER AND SOCIAL MOVEMENT LEADER (1869–1948)

"To find harmony in continual conflict is the key."
—KONOSUKE MATSUSHITA, FOUNDER OF PANASONIC (1894–1989)

"When two men in business always agree, one of them is unnecessary."
—WILLIAM WRIGLEY JR., AMERICAN INDUSTRIALIST (1861–1932)

KNOW THE DIFFERENCE BETWEEN WHAT IS REAL AND WHAT IS FAKE.

Dave Thomas, founder of Wendy's (1932–2002)

This story takes place when Dave Thomas was working as the head chef at an Indiana restaurant. One day a large car drove up to the restaurant and an older gentleman stepped out. It was Colonel Sanders. He asked to be allowed to cook in Dave Thomas's kitchen because he had a secret chicken recipe. Many other chefs had turned down the Colonel's request, but Dave cheerfully agreed. The Colonel's chicken wasn't just good, it was "finger-licking good," and it won over the restaurant owner, too. As a result, the owner bought out some of the Colonel's failing KFC franchises, which were on the verge of bankruptcy, and put Thomas in charge of getting the restaurants back on track. It was Thomas who introduced the familiar red and white bucket to KFC, and he eventually received $1 million for his work. Several years later, Thomas used that money to fund his own hamburger chain, Wendy's.

Keeping an eye out for the real thing can make a positive change in your life.

"Men often applaud an imitation and hiss the real thing."
—AESOP, GREEK STORYTELLER (C. 620–564 BC)

"A jewel, even though it falls into the mud, remains valuable; dust, even though it goes up to the sky, remains worthless."
—SAADI, PERSIAN POET (1184–1291)

"The key to living well in this age is authenticity."
—KONOSUKE MATSUSHITA, FOUNDER OF PANASONIC (1894–1989)

Dustin Hoffman, American actor (1937–)

When he was a child, famed Hollywood actor Dustin Hoffman remembered seeing Humphrey Bogart at the Academy Awards. He later told a journalist that he admired Bogart because he had read that his distinctive way of talking came from an injury he sustained in the war and that he "wanted to find the Humphrey Bogart inside me."

Some people may think that originality is some kind of special talent that comes from heaven. But by imitating the greats and absorbing that information, you can create an originality of your own.

"Those who do not want to imitate anything, produce nothing."
—SALVADOR DALÍ, SPANISH ARTIST (1904–1989)

"Only a fool learns from his own mistakes. The wise man learns from the mistakes of others."
—OTTO VON BISMARCK, PRUSSIAN STATESMAN (1815–1898)

"Employ your time in improving yourself by other men's writings, so that you shall gain easily what others have labored hard for."
—SOCRATES, GREEK PHILOSOPHER (470/469–399 BC)

Tiger Woods, American golfer (1975–)

Tiger Woods's father was great at turning golf practice into a game. When Tiger was a boy, he would spend hours doing a putting contest. His father would place a golf ball three feet from the hole and see who could make the most putts in a row. Once, Tiger sunk seventy putts in a row while his father stood beaming with pride. After their practice, they went back to the clubhouse and celebrated their hard work together—Tiger with a cherry Coke and his father with a beer. Tiger is grateful that his father brought him up this way, saying that the best thing about practicing with his father was that it taught him to enjoy golf. We learn quickly when we are having fun.

A person can grow a lot from a friendly competition.

"Competition is necessary for all endeavors, because our endeavors are born out of competition."
—EIICHI SHIBUSAWA, JAPANESE INDUSTRIALIST (1840–1931)

"I have been up against tough competition all my life. I wouldn't know how to get along without it."
—WALT DISNEY, FOUNDER OF THE WALT DISNEY COMPANY (1901–1966)

"Assume you can learn from everyone, even your 'worst' competitors."
—SAM WALTON, FOUNDER OF WALMART (1918–1992)

THERE IS A ROLE FOR EVERY COLOR.

Konosuke Matsushita, founder of Panasonic (1894–1989)

Konosuke Matsushita was known as "the god of management" because he understood human behavior so well. When his managerial colleagues opposed his decision to appoint an employee who was a hothead and a lush to head an important, cutting-edge business venture, Matsushita responded by saying, "Yes, he has his faults, but a man who works hard also needs to play hard. Take away his enjoyment and he will no longer work hard." But Matsushita was not only focused on creating a team of people with highly charged personalities. He knew that such a team could not thrive, so at the same time he increasingly gave opportunities to the people who at first glance seemed to lack potential. He was known to say to his colleagues, "All of my employees are exceptional to me. They can learn more than I can, and they have great abilities."

Everyone has a role that only they can play. When we discover those roles, we can build a stronger team together.

"Every individual nature has individualist beauty."

—RALPH WALDO EMERSON, AMERICAN ESSAYIST (1803–1882)

"Your first and foremost job as a leader is to take charge of your own energy and then help to orchestrate the energy of those around you."

—PETER DRUCKER, AUSTRIAN BUSINESS-MANAGEMENT SCHOLAR (1909–2005)

"Know each other's strengths and weaknesses, and complement the weaknesses. That is how your shared work will grow and develop."

—KONOSUKE MATSUSHITA, FOUNDER OF PANASONIC (1894–1989)

**Shirase Nobu, Japanese Army officer
and Antarctic explorer (1861–1946)**

Shirase Nobu was the first Japanese person to arrive on the Antarctic continent. Although he is well known in Japan today for bringing his two dogs, Taro and Jiro, on the expedition, people ridiculed him at the time, saying he was crazy for wanting to sail to the South Pole in a fishing boat. On top of that, the support he received from the government for his military service was too small to live off of. So when he decided to go on his expedition to the South Pole, he sold everything he owned, including his house and his military uniform and sword. When the world-famous Norwegian explorer Roald Amundsen went to Japan to see Shirase, the latter had nothing to wear to the meeting, and, by some accounts, went in his bathrobe. But this did not deter him because he held on firmly to his dreams and lived his life to the fullest.

Many people say, "Do what you love," but we often get caught up in the daily struggle to make a living. So every now and then, it's important to take a step back and ask yourself whether you are doing something you truly love.

"I've always been bored with just making money. I've wanted to do things; I wanted to build things, to get things going. What money meant to me was that I was able to get money to do that for me."
—WALT DISNEY, FOUNDER OF THE WALT DISNEY COMPANY (1901–1966)

"The companion of people is not money. Our companions are always people."
—ALEXANDER PUSHKIN, RUSSIAN AUTHOR (1799–1837)

"Money is a great servant but a bad master."
—FRANCIS BACON, ENGLISH PHILOSOPHER (1561–1626)

Marie Curie, Polish physicist and chemist (1867–1934)

Marie Curie truly gave herself to her research. It is estimated that over her forty years of research she was exposed to around two hundred sieverts (a unit of radiation absorption), which is around 600 million times more than the average person is exposed to. From eight years of doing experiments to extract radium, her hands and fingers developed severe burns. The burns on her right hand were particularly harsh, and as a result she lost the ability to hold a pen. To relieve some of her pain, she would constantly rub her fingers together. When she was invited to a reception at the Royal Institution in London after successfully isolating radium, she was unable to fasten her dress because of the pain in her fingers.

There may be only a few people who would endure the kind of pain Marie Curie did for her work, but truly great work can be accomplished only by having the tenacity and determination to make sacrifices.

QUOTES OF THE GREATS

"You cannot know the meaning of 'success' until you have experienced great sacrifice and struggle."

—MAHATMA GANDHI, INDIAN LAWYER AND SOCIAL MOVEMENT LEADER (1869–1948)

"Men challenge their fates. If we do not offer everything and expose ourselves to danger one time, then we can never obtain the prize of great happiness and great freedom."

—HENRY DE MONTHERLANT, FRENCH AUTHOR (1895–1972)

"Knowing that you should get rid of something, that is knowledge. Having the strength and clarity to get rid of something when it must be gotten rid of, that is courage."

—WILHELM MÜLLER, GERMAN POET (1794–1827)

Takasugi Shinsaku, Chōshū samurai (1839–1867)

After the Chōshū Domain of Japan lost its battle against the West, Takasugi Shinsaku was selected as the peace negotiator. At the negotiation table, British admiral Augustus Kuper proposed that the British take control of Hikoshima Island off the southern tip of what is now Yamaguchi Prefecture. Takasugi was infuriated by this proposal, having seen the situation in Shanghai, which was under Western control at the time, where Chinese people were treated inhumanely and were openly refused access to shops and establishments. Takasugi feared that Japan would share the same fate as Shanghai if parts of it fell to Western control. Takasugi approached the negotiations with a tenacity that could cut his opponents but could also ruin himself. Kuper buckled under the pressure from Takasugi and gave up his pursuit of Hikoshima Island. Some still say that if Takasugi had not stood up to Kuper and refused to give up Hikoshima Island, Japan would not have rapidly become the modernized country it is today.

We value maintaining harmony with others, but it can also be necessary to firmly disagree and stand up for what you believe in.

QUOTES OF THE GREATS

"A 'No' uttered from the deepest conviction is better than a 'Yes' merely uttered to please, or worse, to avoid trouble."

—MAHATMA GANDHI, INDIAN LAWYER AND SOCIAL MOVEMENT LEADER (1869–1948)

"If evil flourishes in the world, it is because we lack the courage to say 'No.' "

—SAMUEL SMILES, SCOTTISH AUTHOR (1812–1904)

"To disagree comfortably is to give half of a gift."

—FRIEDRICH BOUTERWEK, GERMAN PHILOSOPHER (1766–1828)

APOLOGIES SHOULD COME FROM THE BOTTOM OF YOUR HEART.

**Abraham Lincoln, sixteenth president
of the United States (1809–1865)**

When Abraham Lincoln was twenty years old he worked at a part-time job. One day after business was over, he counted the day's sales and realized that a customer had overpaid by three cents. He looked over the receipts, trying to think of each customer who had come to the shop. When he realized who had overpaid, he rushed out of the shop and ran down the street after the unsuspecting customer. After running for an hour, he arrived at the customer's house, knocked at the door, and said, "I am so sorry for not noticing," as he handed over the three cents. The woman was moved by his gesture and told him, "Don't ever forget this feeling." Lincoln's relentless sincerity no doubt made him one of America's greatest presidents.

A sincere and honest heart has the power to move others.

"Words and actions that come from a sincere and honest heart are themselves priceless, and will touch the hearts of others."
—KONOSUKE MATSUSHITA, FOUNDER OF PANASONIC (1894–1989)

"The successful man will profit from his mistakes and try again in a different way."
—DALE CARNEGIE, AMERICAN WRITER (1888–1955)

"One of the hardest things in this world is to admit you are wrong. And nothing is more helpful in resolving a situation than its frank admission."
—BENJAMIN DISRAELI, BRITISH POLITICIAN (1804–1881)

Larry Page and Sergey Brin, cofounders of Google (both 1973–)

The cofounders of Google, Larry Page and Sergey Brin, met at Stanford. Although they were not immediately great friends, they agreed that there should be a better way to search for information on the Internet, and they came together to work on their research. They became so absorbed in their project that they dropped out of Stanford and cofounded Google in 1998. They rented the garage of a friend's house and practically lived there while they worked on their research. According to their former professors at Stanford, the two were not exceptional students, but what set them apart was their bold ambition. What enabled them to accomplish such ambitious achievements was finding a partner with a common struggle.

Having friends to share your free time with is important, but a friend who shares your struggle will bring great things into your life.

"Work makes companionship."

—JOHANN WOLFGANG VON GOETHE, GERMAN AUTHOR (1749–1832)

"Friendships multiply joys and divide griefs."

—THOMAS FULLER, ENGLISH PREACHER AND SCHOLAR (1608–1661)

"Men can provide for their wants much more easily by mutual help, and only by uniting their forces can they escape from the dangers that beset them."

—BARUCH SPINOZA, DUTCH PHILOSOPHER (1632–1677)

ADVENTURE

· · · · · · · · · · · · · ·

Mark Twain, American author (1835–1910)

The American novelist Mark Twain is best known for writing *The Adventures of Tom Sawyer* but was at one time a freelance writer. During that time, he knew of a travel tour that went to the World's Fair in Paris, crossed the Mediterranean Sea, and stopped in Egypt. However, only the wealthy could afford to take part in such a tour, which cost too much for a mere freelance writer such as Mark Twain. But he wanted to go on a great adventure so badly that he implored a local newspaper to let him go, promising to send an article from each of the fifty places he would visit. The newspaper agreed and paid for the full cost of his travels. The articles he wrote during his travels were later published in a highly acclaimed book. The novels that Twain perfected in his later years feature a fresh and vibrant spirit of adventure, which undoubtedly grew out of those travels.

Travel can open our eyes to amazing things that we never imagined. It is not always easy to plan a trip, but sometimes you have to go out of your way a little bit to see the world.

"Travel is the greatest source of true knowledge."
—BENJAMIN DISRAELI, BRITISH POLITICIAN (1804–1881)

"For I assure you, without travel, at least for people from the arts and sciences, one is a miserable creature!"
—WOLFGANG AMADEUS MOZART, AUSTRIAN COMPOSER (1756–1791)

"It is good to have an end to journey toward, but it is the journey that matters in the end."
—URSULA K. LE GUIN, AMERICAN FANTASY AUTHOR (1929–)

QUOTES OF THE GREATS

ONLY BY STRETCHING
YOURSELF WILL YOU SEE A NEW VIEW.

Steven Spielberg, American film director (1946–)

For years, there was a widely told (and now discredited) story about how the world-renowned film director Steven Spielberg got his start in the movie business. Though most sources now acknowledge this tale as apocryphal, it still speaks to the power of big dreams (and, perhaps, the birth of an epic storyteller). While still a college student, Spielberg was shooting an independent film and decided he wanted to see a real film set. So, he went on a tour of Universal Studios. Halfway through the tour, he quietly got out of the tour vehicle and hid inside the studio until the tour was over. Afterward, he changed into a suit and carried a briefcase as though he worked there. He talked to and befriended actual employees, and even found an empty room, wrote his name on a placard, and used it as his office. A tall tale, to be sure—but a powerful reminder to always think big!

When we take bold actions, we may fail or feel embarrassed sometimes. But bold actions that challenge our limits can take us to new places and give us a new perspective.

QUOTES OF THE GREATS

"Always dream and shoot higher than you know you can do. Don't bother just to be better than your contemporaries or predecessors. Try to be better than yourself."
—WILLIAM FAULKNER, AMERICAN NOVELIST (1897–1962)

"People never improve unless they look to some standard or example higher or better than themselves."
—TRYON EDWARDS, AMERICAN THEOLOGIAN (1809–1894)

"Every man takes the limits of his own field of vision for the limits of the world."
—ARTHUR SCHOPENHAUER, GERMAN PHILOSOPHER (1788–1860)

**Florence Nightingale, English social reformer
and pioneer of modern nursing (1820–1910)**

Known as the White Angel, Florence Nightingale was so driven by her conviction to take care of wounded soldiers on the battlefield that she gave up everything else. Although she was born into a wealthy landowning family, she summarily refused the proposals of multiple suitors, saying that she could not be a nurse if she became a nobleman's wife. After her reputation as a nurse had grown, requests for her lectures and speeches poured in. But she turned all the requests down and devoted herself to writing so that she could pass on everything she had learned about nursing to those in training.

We may not all have such strong convictions as Florence Nightingale had, but we should not be afraid to step out of a comfortable, protected place and live our dreams.

"Life is an adventure; dare it."
—MOTHER TERESA, ROMAN CATHOLIC MISSIONARY (1910–1997)

"And you all know, security is mortals' chiefest enemy."
—WILLIAM SHAKESPEARE, ENGLISH PLAYWRIGHT (1564–1616)

"Men are not prisoners of fate, but only prisoners of their own minds."
—FRANKLIN D. ROOSEVELT, THIRTY-SECOND PRESIDENT OF THE UNITED STATES
(1882–1945)

QUOTES OF THE GREATS

NO NEED TO HOLD BACK.

Mikimoto Kōkichi, founder of Mikimoto (1858–1954)

Mikimoto Kōkichi enjoyed great success for creating the first cultured pearls and for turning his name into a world-renowned luxury brand. While he was still working hard at cultivating pearl oysters, he made a pilgrimage to the Ise Grand Shrine. He paid homage at the shrine and thought, *How can I create a pearl that has the beauty of a natural pearl?* Lost in thought, he accidentally placed fifty *sen*—a great sum of money in today's currency—into the offering box. Any other person would have left the money in the box, but Mikimoto went to a shrine guard and asked to have his money returned. The guard refused, saying that although he had no reason to doubt Mikimoto, he had never had such a request before. But Mikimoto persisted, and eventually the guard returned his money. For Mikimoto, the embarrassment of making such a request was outweighed by the value that the money had toward his successful cultivation of pearls. In fact, he invested that money into his research, and after his success donated large sums of money to the Ise Grand Shrine in return for the kindness he was shown there.

There is no need to hold back when you know what your priorities are. Have confidence in choosing the best option.

QUOTES OF THE GREATS

"What do I regret the most? It is that I always held back and never listened to my own true feelings."
—FRIEDRICH NIETZSCHE, GERMAN PHILOSOPHER (1844–1900)

"Your playing small does not serve the world. There is nothing enlightened about shrinking so that other people won't feel insecure around you."
—MARIANNE WILLIAMSON, AMERICAN SPIRITUAL TEACHER AND AUTHOR (1952–)

"The world is opening up to you. Proceed without fear or reservation. The land stretches expansively and the sky stretches into infinity."
—JOHANN WOLFGANG VON GOETHE, GERMAN AUTHOR (1749–1832)

Johann Sebastian Bach, German composer (1685–1750)

Composer Johann Sebastian Bach had several children to support. In order to bring in extra income, Bach actively took on extra work in addition to his main job. Other composers' pride made them choose carefully which work they took on, but Bach would take on whatever came his way. For example, he wrote the music for the funerals of distinguished people of the city, and even wrote an operetta called *The Coffee Cantata* that praised the benefits of coffee—a new drink at the time. This broad body of work had a great effect on other composers, so much so that Bach later came to be called "the Father of Music."

If you cling to a rigid image of yourself, you will close yourself off from many opportunities. Challenge yourself by actively seeking experiences in fields you have yet to explore.

"What is necessary to change a person is to change his awareness of himself."

—ABRAHAM MASLOW, AMERICAN PSYCHOLOGIST (1908–1970)

"Abandonment is the key to innovation."

—PETER DRUCKER, AUSTRIAN BUSINESS-MANAGEMENT SCHOLAR (1909–2005)

"The bird fights its way out of the egg. The egg is the world. Who would be born must first destroy a world."

—HERMANN HESSE, GERMAN AUTHOR (1877–1962)

A PATH YOU CAN'T GIVE UP.

Richard Bach, American author and aviator (1936–)

Richard Bach dreamed of flying freely through the sky, and so he dropped out of college and joined the air force. However, he learned that young people were not allowed to pilot planes, and he left the military after two years. Next, he joined a private airline company and became a pilot just like he had dreamed. But, failing to find the freedom he had been dreaming of, he quit after eleven months. But he kept pursuing his dream of flying freely in the sky like a bird. He wrote the book *Jonathan Livingston Seagull*, which featured a seagull as the main character, and became a bestselling author. Richard Bach said this: "Choose a love and work to make it true, and somehow something will happen, something you couldn't plan."

When you feel a strong determination within yourself, there is no need to compromise with others. Stay true to your convictions and don't be misled by your surroundings.

"**Accomplishments will prove to be a journey, not a destination.**"
—DWIGHT D. EISENHOWER, THIRTY-FOURTH PRESIDENT OF THE UNITED STATES (1890–1969)

"**Someone said to me, 'If fifty percent of the experts in Hollywood said you had no talent and should give up, what would you do?' My answer was then and still is, 'If a hundred percent told me that, all one hundred percent would be wrong.'**"
—MARILYN MONROE, AMERICAN ACTRESS (1926–1962)

"**There are many thorns along the path that I go. Be that as it may, there is only one path of life. There is no other path; I shall go down this one.**"
—MUSHANOKŌJI SANEATSU, JAPANESE NOVELIST (1885–1976)

Galileo Galilei, Italian physicist and astronomer (1564–1642)

Galileo became famous for his work on Copernican theory, and was known as a fighter in his younger days because of his tendency to speak frankly. When Galileo was attending university in Pisa, he would challenge the professors there who would give only secondhand accounts of the established wisdom of the day. As a prime example, he criticized Aristotle's theory of falling objects, which said that heavier objects will fall faster than lighter objects, a theory that not a single person doubted at the time. Later, he was indicted by the Inquisition for his writings on Copernican theory, and all his writings on the subject were banned. In 1632, he published the *Dialogue Concerning the Two Chief World Systems* and was again called by the Inquisition, and this time he was placed under house arrest. However, he persisted, and in 1638, he secretly completed his great work the *Discourses and Mathematical Demonstrations Relating to Two New Sciences.* Galileo spent the rest of his life fighting in this way, challenging and tarnishing the established wisdom.

When you feel that organizations and systems are flawed, don't grumble quietly in the shadows; you have to shout it with conviction.

"Do not fear. Trust in the little voice that echoes in your heart."

—MAHATMA GANDHI, INDIAN LAWYER AND SOCIAL MOVEMENT LEADER (1869–1948)

" 'Tis the business of little minds to shrink; but he whose heart is firm, and whose conscience approves his conduct, will pursue his principles unto death."

—THOMAS PAINE, ENGLISH POLITICAL THEORIST (1737–1809)

"There is no week nor day nor hour when tyranny may not enter upon this country, if the people lose their roughness and spirit of defiance."

—WALT WHITMAN, AMERICAN POET (1819–1892)

QUOTES OF THE GREATS

· 33 ·
BE HUNGRY.

Ernest Thompson Seton, English natural historian (1860–1946)

Ernest Seton, who is known for writing *Wild Animals I Have Known*, dreamed of becoming a natural historian when he was a schoolboy. While attending school in England, he heard that the library of the British Museum (Natural History) was hosting a collection of natural history books from all over the world. His heart raced as his feet carried him to the museum. But when he got there, he was refused entry because he was too young; minors were not allowed inside. Seton went and appealed directly to the museum director, who also refused to let him in, saying that if the other museum trustees consented it would not be a problem to let young Seton enter the museum, but because they were not around it was not possible. But Seton was not discouraged, and he wrote a letter to each of the trustees that expressed his great passion to enter the museum. Two weeks later, Seton was allowed in under special permission. Seton also received encouragement from the trustees, who wrote back urging him to pursue his studies with utmost effort.

Be greedy in pursuing your goals. If you do, the path to success will surely open up.

"The characteristic of a truly able man is that he is never satisfied with himself."
—PLAUTUS, ROMAN PLAYWRIGHT (C. 254–184 BC)

"Better to be Socrates dissatisfied than a fool satisfied."
—JOHN STUART MILL, ENGLISH POLITICAL ECONOMIST (1806–1873)

"Restlessness is discontent and discontent is the first necessity of progress. Show me a thoroughly satisfied man and I will show you a failure."
—THOMAS EDISON, AMERICAN INDUSTRIALIST AND INVENTOR (1847–1931)

34

THE WORLD CANNOT BE EXPERIENCED THROUGH THE INTERNET

Jean-Henri Fabre, French entomologist (1823–1915)

Jean-Henri Fabre is best known as an early entomologist, but he was originally a teacher. Thoughout his entire life, Fabre was fascinated by plant and insect specimens but often observed them only in the lab. One day, prompted by a discussion of the jewel beetle in a magazine, Fabre realized he wanted to observe live insects directly in nature and unravel their mystery. Afterward, he wrote *Fabre's Book of Insects*, which was based on his observations of insects in their natural habitats. Fabre's methods for observing insect behavior had a great influence on the future development of scientific methods.

Real knowledge comes from direct experience. Take every chance to experience things in the real world.

"One's own experience, no matter how small, is an asset more valuable than the experience of a million other people."
—GOTTHOLD EPHRAIM LESSING, GERMAN WRITER AND PHILOSOPHER (1729–1781)

"There are many truths of which the full meaning cannot be realized until personal experience has brought it home."
—JOHN STUART MILL, ENGLISH POLITICAL ECONOMIST (1806–1873)

"Open the door. There is a vast world out there."
—SAKICHI TOYODA, FOUNDER OF TOYOTA GROUP (1867–1930)

35

DANCE YOUR OWN DANCE.

Jippensha Ikku, Edo period fiction writer (1765–1831)

Jippensha Ikku, who is best known for his picaresque novel *Tokaidōchū Hizakurige* (*Shank's Mare*), was determined to live solely as a writer, and so spent his entire life in poverty. While living day-to-day in tenement housing, Ikku was forced to pawn what little furniture he owned. But he did not fall into despair. On the bare walls of his house he hung pictures of vases, bookshelves, and tables, creating the illusion of a completely different room. Someone entering his house for the first time would have mistaken the pictures on the walls for the real thing, and would have let out a hearty laugh at the surprising realization that his eyes had deceived him.

Even if you find yourself in difficult circumstances, find the humor and strength to live freely.

QUOTES OF THE GREATS

"The habit of being happy enables one to be freed, or largely freed, from the domination of outward conditions."
—ROBERT LOUIS STEVENSON, SCOTTISH NOVELIST (1850–1894)

"I prefer the folly of enthusiasm to the indifference of wisdom."
—ANATOLE FRANCE, FRENCH POET (1844–1924)

"A confident, self-taught style is better than a faithless orthodoxy."
—ARNOLD PALMER, AMERICAN GOLFER (1929–)

36

EXPLORE THE "UNDISCOVERED" PATH.

Frederick W. Smith, founder of FedEx (1944–)

Federal Express operates in more than 215 countries worldwide and has over six hundred delivery aircraft, making it the world's largest freight delivery company. The idea for FedEx came quickly to founder Frederick W. Smith, who submitted the proposal in a report for his college economics class. However, the professor did not evaluate Smith's proposal favorably, and gave it a C. Smith ignored his professor's low evaluation and created the swift parcel delivery system known as FedEx. In fact, the report that Smith wrote in college is now on display at the company's headquarters.

The newer and more radical an idea is, the fewer people there are to accurately evaluate it. Don't worry about what others may think, and create the path to do what no one else has done before.

"If you want to succeed, you should strike out on new paths, rather than travel the worn paths of accepted success."
—JOHN D. ROCKEFELLER, AMERICAN INDUSTRIALIST AND PHILANTHROPIST (1839–1937)

"For actually the earth had no roads to begin with, but when many men pass one way, a road is made."
—LU XUN, CHINESE POET (1881–1936)

"We keep moving forward, opening new doors, and doing new things because we're curious, and curiosity keeps leading us down new paths."
—WALT DISNEY, FOUNDER OF THE WALT DISNEY COMPANY (1901–1966)

RELAX

· · · · · · · · · · · · · · · · ·

Albert Einstein, German physicist (1879–1955)

The Institute for Advanced Study in Princeton, New Jersey, is one of the most famous research institutes in the United States. It is where Albert Einstein worked as a researcher from 1933 until his death in 1955. A story is often told there of how the other researchers would be working diligently at their research as the sound of an out-of-tune violin would come seeping out from Einstein's office. It was Einstein who was playing the violin, which he often did when he had reached the limits of his research.

It's important to work hard and stick to your goals, but sometimes we also need to relax for a moment and loosen up our shoulders.

"Our minds must have relaxation: rested, they will rise up better and keener."
—LUCIUS ANNAEUS SENECA, ROMAN PHILOSOPHER (C. 4 **BC–AD** 65)

"Eat a little, drink a little, and then take a quick rest. That is the panacea for the whole world."
—EUGÈNE DELACROIX, FRENCH ARTIST (1798–1863)

"A person who is tired should rest for a moment in the grass by the roadside and watch the people who travel down the road. They probably won't go very far."
—IVAN TURGENEV, RUSSIAN NOVELIST (1818–1883)

QUOTES OF THE GREATS

Johannes Gutenberg, German goldsmith and printer (c. 1395–1468)

Before Johannes Gutenberg's invention of the printing press, every book had to be written by hand. Gutenberg hoped that his printing press would make a vast amount of knowledge available to a great number of people, but he also feared that the printing press would make it easy to print books of no value. Because of these fears, Gutenberg did not release the plans for his printing press publicly for many years. However, after many long years passed, Gutenberg finally released his press publicly. It made a great contribution to the cultural revolution that followed, and is considered one of the most important inventions of the Renaissance.

Great results are born out of dealing with what actually happens when you do something, rather than worrying about what might happen if you do something.

"I've had a lot of worries in my life, most of which never happened."
—MARK TWAIN, AMERICAN AUTHOR (1835–1910)

"If I think hard about something for three hours and think that I have come to the right conclusion, my mind will not change even if I think on it for another three years."
—FRANKLIN D. ROOSEVELT, THIRTY-SECOND PRESIDENT OF THE UNITED STATES (1882–1945)

"There are no desperate situations; there are only desperate people."
—HEINZ WILHELM GUDERIAN, GERMAN GENERAL (1888–1954)

IT'S GOOD TO SPLURGE FROM TIME TO TIME.

Richard Branson, founder of Virgin Group (1950–)

The top businessmen and entrepreneurs often live in large mansions, but Richard Branson acquired his mansion at quite a young age—when he was only twenty-one years old, in 1971. While casually flipping through a magazine, he instantly fell in love with a sixteenth-century mansion. He did everything he could—haggle on the price, borrow money from his grandmother—in order to buy the mansion. After he had acquired the mansion, he quickly set out to remodel it into a recording studio, where he recorded great hits by Paul and Linda McCartney, the Rolling Stones, Boy George, and other top artists.

Saving money is important, but don't spare any expenses for the things that have true value.

"There are certainly things in our lives that are unnecessary, but it is because of these unnecessary things that our emotions are born, that we can find profit, and that our hearts are softened."
—SHŪSAKU ENDŌ, JAPANESE NOVELIST AND ESSAYIST (1923–1996)

"The time you enjoy wasting is not wasted time."
—BERTRAND RUSSELL, BRITISH PHILOSOPHER (1872–1970)

"Luxury need not have a price—comfort itself is a luxury."
—GEOFFREY BEENE, AMERICAN FASHION DESIGNER (1927–2004)

QUOTES OF THE GREATS

Soichiro Honda, founder of Honda (1906–1991)

Soichiro Honda spent his life doing the things he wanted to do, living frankly and unapologetically. Just before his death, he called out to his wife and asked her to carry him on her back and walk around the hospital room. She obliged her husband, carrying him on her back and slowly walking around as his IV tubes swayed back and forth. When she had finished, Soichiro passed away with these last words: "I am satisfied." Soichiro's close friend and cofounder of Sony, Masaru Ibuka, said that Honda was able to do the things he wanted to during his life because of how much he loved and depended on his wife, and that he must have felt great satisfaction in that love and dependence right until the end of his life. Surely the real request that he made to his wife on his deathbed was to feel her loving touch one last time.

Humans are creatures who long for another's touch more than their words.

"If you smile at one hundred people, then you will soften one hundred hearts; if you hold the hands of one hundred people, then you will feel their warmth one hundred times."
—MOTHER TERESA, ROMAN CATHOLIC MISSIONARY (1910–1997)

"Working mothers should hold their children for at least eight seconds before they leave the house."
—MASARU IBUKA, COFOUNDER OF SONY (1908–1997)

"The hands of those I meet are dumbly eloquent to me."
—HELEN KELLER, POLITICAL ACTIVIST (1880–1968)

41

WASH AWAY WHAT IS ALREADY DONE.

Robert the Bruce, King of Scots (1274–1329)

Robert the Bruce, King of Scots, fought many battles against the English and lost many times. After one defeat, he rode off from his vassals and entered a deep cave alone. In his despair, he thought that his family's reign would be over. Then, from the corner of his eye, he saw a single spider. The spider was trying to build its web, but a strong wind prevented the spider from attaching the silken thread to its destination. Robert watched as the spider tried three times and failed three times. *You feel the bitter cruelty of failure just as I do*, Robert thought. But then he saw the spider try to build its web a fourth time, and it was successful. It is said that at the sight of the spider's success, a flame of passion sparked in Robert's heart to fight again to restore his crown.

When you become a prisoner of your failures, you lose the strength to fight. Wash away what is already done and face a new challenge.

"Time heals all wounds."

—CICERO, ROMAN STATESMAN (106–43 BC)

"A retentive memory may be a good thing, but the ability to forget is the true token of greatness."

—ELBERT HUBBARD, AMERICAN WRITER AND PUBLISHER (1856–1915)

"Wise men do not have time to think much on matters past because their hands are full thinking only of the present and the future."

—FRANCIS BACON, ENGLISH PHILOSOPHER (1561–1626)

42

PLACE TEMPTATIONS OUT OF SIGHT.

William Smith Clark, American educator (1826–1886)

William S. Clark is best known for saying "Boys, be ambitious!" He worked as the head of the Sapporo Agricultural College in Sapporo, Japan, where there was an ongoing problem with students drinking alcohol and getting into trouble that Clark could not fix. Clark tried to warn the students, but he seemed to lack the persuasive power to change their behavior. But Clark also liked to drink alcohol himself, and had in fact already received a year's supply of wine from the United States. Clark decided to set an example for his students, so he took all the bottles of wine, lined them up in front of the students, and broke each one, saying, "You all need to control yourselves!" After that, there were no more incidents involving drunken students.

It's best to take the things that interfere with your goals and put them out of sight.

"I count him braver who overcomes his desires than him who conquers his enemies; for the hardest victory is over self."
—ARISTOTLE, GREEK PHILOSOPHER (384–322 BC)

"There is no shame for the man who loses to his struggles; rather, there is shame in losing to pleasure."
—BLAISE PASCAL, FRENCH PHILOSOPHER (1623–1662)

"I can think of nothing less pleasurable than a life devoted to pleasure."
—JOHN D. ROCKEFELLER, AMERICAN INDUSTRIALIST AND PHILANTHROPIST (1839–1937)

43

LET'S STOP BEING WASTEFUL.

**John D. Rockefeller, American industrialist
and philanthropist (1839–1937)**

Even after Rockefeller made his fortune in the oil industry, he continued to have lunch at the same cheap restaurant. He would order the same meal every time, and after he had finished he would pay the thirty-five-cent bill and tip the waiter fifteen cents. But one day the waiter brought back incorrect change, and in order to teach the waiter a lesson, Rockefeller took ten cents off the tip. The waiter protested, saying, "If I were as rich as you are, I wouldn't be so stingy over ten cents." Rockefeller replied, "If you really valued this ten cents, you wouldn't have miscalculated my change, and you would be earning a better salary than you are now."

Value your money, and value your possessions. This is the habit of successful people of every era.

"Beware of little expenses; a small leak will sink a great ship."
—BENJAMIN FRANKLIN, AMERICAN WRITER AND STATESMAN (1706–1790)

"Without frugality none can be rich, and with it very few would be poor."
—SAMUEL JOHNSON, ENGLISH WRITER (1709–1784)

"A small profit watched carefully will become a large fortune."
—HAN FEI, CHINESE THINKER (280–233 BC)

William Gladstone, British politician (1809–1898)

William Gladstone hated math when he was at university, and wrote a letter to his father asking that he be transferred to a university without math. His father was a member of Parliament and could have arranged for his son's transfer, but instead wrote him back, saying, "You say that you dislike math, but there is a supreme pleasure to be found in putting all of your efforts into a subject that you dislike. You may be faced with a time in your future when you must overcome your weaknesses. This will be a great practice for such a time when you will overcome even greater obstacles." Gladstone, reflecting on his political career, which continued until he was eighty-five years old, during which he served four times as prime minister, said that "if I had not received my father's advice during my university days, I would not have become the person that I am today."

It is important to build your strengths, but it is just as important to experience the exhilaration of overcoming your weaknesses. That will bring you an even greater advantage.

"A man's greatest strength develops at the point where he overcomes his greatest weakness."
—ELMER G. LETERMAN, AMERICAN INSURANCE SALESMAN (1897–1982)

"I always feel happiness when I overcome any difficulty."
—LUDWIG VAN BEETHOVEN, GERMAN COMPOSER (1770–1827)

"My attitude is that if you push me towards something that you think is a weakness, then I will turn that perceived weakness into a strength."
—MICHAEL JORDAN, AMERICAN BASKETBALL PLAYER (1963–)

45

LOOK OBJECTIVELY AT YOURSELF.

Howard Schultz, CEO of Starbucks (1953–)

In 2008, Starbucks CEO Howard Schultz took a frank and honest look at his company's performance and saw that Starbucks was beginning to lose its romantic, dramatic character. In order to stop this trend, he thought, the company needed to get back to its core principles. So one Tuesday Schultz closed all 7,100 Starbucks stores—forfeiting over $6 million in revenue—and held seminars to teach each of the 135,000 baristas how to make the perfect espresso. As a result, Starbucks' stock value increased by a record percentage over the next several years.

We all need to have the courage to take an objective look at ourselves. That courage itself will lead us down a path of new growth.

"Almost all our misfortunes in life come from the wrong notions we have about the things that happen to us."
—STENDHAL, FRENCH WRITER (1783–1842)

"He knows the universe and does not know himself."
—JEAN DE LA FONTAINE, FRENCH POET (1621–1695)

"The mirror holds the brew of pretension, but at the same time holds the antidote to pride."
—NATSUME SŌSEKI, JAPANESE NOVELIST AND SCHOLAR (1867–1916)

46

UNABLE TO PERFORM BEYOND WHAT YOU'VE PRACTICED.

**Franklin D. Roosevelt, thirty-second president
of the United States (1882–1945)**

President Roosevelt was a master at making public speeches. When he was asked by a reporter to make an address, he said, "There are twenty hours between now and tomorrow, so I should be able to give a fifteen-minute speech." The reporter was puzzled and asked whether the president truly needed twenty hours to prepare for a fifteen-minute speech. President Roosevelt replied that it takes one hour to prepare a one-page script, and since one page of script equals one minute of speech, he would need twenty hours including five hours for sleep. Then, true to his word, President Roosevelt canceled all his other appointments and wrote his speech, which moved his audience, as they always did.

A master is not someone who possesses superhuman abilities. A master is a person who prepares meticulously and offers perfect service and care.

QUOTES OF THE GREATS

"Above all, preparation is the key to success."
—HENRY FORD, FOUNDER OF THE FORD MOTOR COMPANY (1863–1947)

"In the fields of observation, chance favors only the prepared mind."
—LOUIS PASTEUR, FRENCH CHEMIST (1822–1895)

"If I don't practice one day, I know it; two days, the critics know it; three days, the public knows it."
—JASCHA HEIFETZ, LITHUANIAN-BORN AMERICAN VIOLINIST (1901–1987)

Pythagoras, Greek mathematician and philosopher (c. 570–c. 495 BC)
This (likely apocryphal, but still lovely) story takes place when the mathematician Pythagoras—famous for the Pythagorean theorem—was walking through town. As he walked, he could hear the sounds of blacksmiths' hammers echoing through the streets, which sometimes sounded pleasant, and other times sounded harsh and discordant. In order to figure out the reason for this, Pythagoras compared the weights of the hammers that the blacksmiths used. He found that when the blacksmiths used hammers whose weights were related by 2:1 or 3:1 ratios, it resulted in a pleasant sound. He theorized that the beautiful ratios were the source of the beautiful sounds. Though this story is likely a myth, Pythagoras's work has had great influence on mathematics and philosophy since his time, and was sometimes inspired in unlikely ways by his own neighborhood.

The places you would never think to look are precisely where new discoveries are waiting to be found.

QUOTES OF THE GREATS

"Surprise is the greatest part of humanity."
—JOHANN WOLFGANG VON GOETHE, GERMAN AUTHOR (1749–1832)

"The real voyage of discovery consists not in seeking new lands but seeing with new eyes."
—MARCEL PROUST, FRENCH AUTHOR (1871–1922)

"To myself I am only a child playing on the beach, while vast oceans of truth lie undiscovered before me."
—ISAAC NEWTON, ENGLISH PHYSICIST AND MATHEMATICIAN (1643–1727)

Tokugawa Ieyasu, Shogun and feudal lord (1543–1616)

Tokugawa Ieyasu, whose shogunate laid the foundation for the Edo period, is said to have possessed knowledge of medicine that put doctors to shame. He is said to have prepared powerful medicines himself and to have cured his grandson Iemitsu's illness even after the doctors had given up hope. Ieyasu valued his health, and would often go swimming and horseback riding, and trained in archery, kendo, and falconry. He is reported to have said that "Falconry allows you to understand the hardships of the lower classes, and trains your body better than any other activity." It was no doubt the high value Ieyasu placed on health and physical activity that enabled him to survive the years he spent during his childhood as a hostage of rival Oda Nobunaga, and allowed him to wait until the right opportunity to challenge then leader Toyotomi Hideyoshi.

You can't neglect your health if you want to achieve your biggest dreams and highest goals.

"The preservation of health is a duty."
—HERBERT SPENCER, ENGLISH PHILOSOPHER (1820–1903)

"What can be added to the happiness of a man who is in health, out of debt, and has a clear conscience?"
—ADAM SMITH, SCOTTISH MORAL PHILOSOPHER AND PIONEER OF POLITICAL ECONOMY (1723–1790)

QUOTES OF THE GREATS

49

A PERSON WHO IS ON TIME IS A PERSON WHO CAN BE TRUSTED.

Benjamin Franklin, American writer and statesman (1706–1790)

One story about Benjamin Franklin tells of his time working as a bookstore owner, when a customer came into the shop and demanded that the clerk give him a discount. The clerk replied that they did not give discounts, and the customer asked to see the owner. When the customer saw Franklin, he said, "Two dollars is too expensive. Give me a discount." Franklin replied, "All right, now the price is two dollars and fifty cents." Surprised, the customer responded, "Don't joke with me. How much is it really?" "It's three dollars now," Franklin said. "Time is money. If it were me, I would have bought the book at two dollars and not wasted my time." The customer understood what Franklin was saying and took out three dollars to buy the book. Franklin stopped the customer, saying, "If you understand my point, then two dollars will be fine," and sold him the book for two dollars.

Benjamin Franklin was famous for his punctuality and always took care not to waste others' time. Time is a priceless asset for all of us.

> **"Punctuality is the politeness of kings."**
> —LOUIS XVIII, KING OF FRANCE (1755–1824)

> **"You are not born for fame if you don't know the value of time."**
> —LUC DE CLAPIERS, MARQUIS DE VAUVENARGUES, FRENCH WRITER AND MORALIST (1715–1747)

> **"Do not delay; the golden moments fly!"**
> —HENRY WADSWORTH LONGFELLOW, AMERICAN POET (1807–1882)

QUOTES OF THE GREATS

50

DON'T SKIP ANY STEPS.

James Garfield, twentieth president of the United States (1831–1881)
When President Garfield was at university there was one particular student in his math class who always received the highest marks. Garfield hated to lose and put all his effort into his studies, but no matter how hard he tried, he could not seem to surpass this student. One night, after Garfield had finished studying and was getting ready for bed, he glanced toward the other student's room and saw that the light was on. After ten minutes the light went out. Suddenly Garfield thought, *That's it. It's that ten minutes.* From the next day Garfield studied ten minutes longer and went to bed ten minutes later than usual, and eventually received the highest grade in his math class. Later, when he reflected on that time in his life while president, he said, "Understanding the value of those ten extra minutes is the key to achieving success in any endeavor."

Results are not to be found in short, quick leaps, but in steady, daily effort. Let's make that our habit.

"Most things can be substituted with something, but there is no substitute for diligence."
—G. KINGSLEY WARD, CANADIAN ENTREPRENEUR (1932–2014)

"There is no road too long to the man who advances deliberately and without undue haste; there are no honors too distant to the man who prepares himself for them with patience."
—JEAN DE LA BRUYÈRE, FRENCH PHILOSOPHER (1645–1696)

"A dullard who tries gets more work done than a genius who doesn't try."
—JOHN AUBREY, ENGLISH AUTHOR (1626–1697)

51

LEND A HAND EVEN TO YOUR ENEMY.

Bill Gates, cofounder of Microsoft (1955–)

In 1997, immediately following Steve Jobs's return to the company, Apple's finances were in trouble. At one point, the company's bank account had only enough money for a few weeks' worth of expenses. But there was one person who offered Apple a helping hand. That person was Bill Gates of Microsoft, Apple's longtime rival. At that time, the two companies were engaged in a legal copyright dispute that had stretched for years, and were not in what one might call a friendly relationship. Even so, Gates agreed to a $150 million investment in Apple and to the development of Microsoft Office software for Apple computers. Gates said that despite their rivalry, he and others at Microsoft liked Apple and its products.

When opponents offer to help each other, they can create new value.

"In taking revenge, a man is but even with his enemy; but in passing it over, he is superior."
—FRANCIS BACON, ENGLISH PHILOSOPHER (1561–1626)

"He who cannot forgive a trespass of malice to his enemy has never yet tasted the most sublime enjoyment of love."
—JOHANN KASPAR LAVATER, SWISS POET AND PHILOSOPHER (1741–1801)

"You cannot shake hands with a clenched fist."
—INDIRA GANDHI, PRIME MINISTER OF INDIA (1917–1984)

52

TOUGH TIMES ARE WHEN ONE IS BEING TESTED.

Nelson Mandela, South African politician (1918–2013)

Nelson Mandela spent twenty-seven years in prison for his opposition to apartheid in South Africa. His cell was smaller than the average person's bathroom—only three steps deep and two and a half steps wide. Despite these conditions, Mandela seized on a good opportunity to closely observe the white men who guarded his cell. *Let me try to work with the guards and win their respect by how I conduct myself. If I can do it here, then I can do the same with white people all over the world.* With that in mind, he cooperated with his white captors in order to understand them well, and he eventually won their respect. After his release from prison, Mandela became the first black president of the Republic of South Africa.

If you are put in harsh circumstances, think of it as a test of your character.

"None but yourself who are your greatest foe."
—HENRY WADSWORTH LONGFELLOW, AMERICAN POET (1807–1882)

"People coddle themselves and are fooled easily."
—NICCOLÒ MACHIAVELLI, ITALIAN DIPLOMAT AND HISTORIAN (1469–1527)

"A man's true strength comes out when he is chased into a corner. From the great many obstacles that I have seen in my life, I can only conclude that destiny is making me stronger."
—FRIEDRICH SCHILLER, GERMAN POET (1759–1805)

QUOTES OF THE GREATS

Mark Spitz, American swimmer (1950–)

When Michael Phelps won six gold medals at the Athens Olympics, the world thought he had reached his limit. But Phelps's coach thought he should keep setting his sights higher, and there was one other person who agreed without hesitation as to Phelps's ability. That was Mark Spitz, who won seven gold medals in the 1972 Olympics. In 2008, everyone agreed, "Phelps is certain to win eight gold medals in the Beijing Olympics," to which Spitz agreed: "Records are made to be broken." And indeed, Phelps went on to win eight gold medals in the Beijing Olympics. In an interview a few years later in *Parade* magazine, Spitz said, "I was honored to witness an athlete of that caliber be so successful."

Mark Spitz has continued to support and encourage many people, and left a great record. We must not forget that we exist to support and give back to one another.

QUOTES OF THE GREATS

"He who has once done you a kindness will be more ready to do you another than he whom you yourself have obliged."
—BENJAMIN FRANKLIN, AMERICAN WRITER AND STATESMAN (1706–1790)

"When you give yourself, you receive more than you give."
—ANTOINE DE SAINT-EXUPÉRY, FRENCH AUTHOR (1900–1944)

"Life is a vineyard we share with others. Together we cultivate it and together we harvest."
—ROMAIN ROLLAND, FRENCH AUTHOR (1866–1944)

COMMUNICATION

· · · · · · · · · · · · · ·

Martin Luther, German theologian (1483–1546)

As founder of the Protestant Reformation, Martin Luther had a profound influence on faith and ideology. Luther said that in order to be a respected preacher, you need to have the following six characteristics: Speak with clear pronunciation. Speak with eloquence. Have extensive knowledge. Give money without taking it. Talk about things that people want to hear. Make a good impression. Even Martin Luther, who spent most of his days in fervent monastic life praying and doing research, understood the importance of first impressions.

Anyone can see that a person's clean appearance and good manners depend on the amount of effort they put into it. By making a good first impression, many people will want to listen to what you have to say.

"Clothes that you wear sometimes represent you."
—G. KINGSLEY WARD, CANADIAN ENTREPRENEUR (1932–2014)

"And then, you never know, maybe that's the day she has a date with destiny. And it's best to be as pretty as possible for destiny."
—COCO CHANEL, FRENCH FASHION DESIGNER (1883–1971)

"The clothing that covers your body and the smile that floats upon your lips reveal your true character."
—OLD TESTAMENT

Sanjugo Naoki, Japanese writer (1891–1934)

When Sanjugo Naoki—for whom the literary Naoki Prize is named—was a young man, he consumed only literature and lived in poverty. Naoki was forced to borrow money, and as a result debt collectors often visited his family home. One day, when three debt collectors came to Naoki's home, he did not give any excuse for his lack of payment and simply sat in silence. After much time had passed, Naoki said to the debt collectors, "I'm starving. Can I borrow some money? We can go eat together." Two of the debt collectors left in anger, but one remained. The remaining debt collector smiled and said, "I guess I have no choice," and treated Naoki to a bowl of udon noodles.

Certainly, it is important not to completely rely on others for everything. But from time to time, having the flexibility to call on others can save us in a pinch.

QUOTES OF THE GREATS

"There are no ugly women; there are only women who do not know how to look pretty."
—PIERRE-ANTOINE BERRYER, FRENCH LAWYER AND POLITICIAN (1790–1868)

"A person without charm is no good, no matter how talented they are."
—KONOSUKE MATSUSHITA, FOUNDER OF PANASONIC (1894–1989)

"We take interest in people who take interest in us."
—PUBLILIUS SYRUS, LATIN WRITER OF MAXIMS (85–43 BC)

Toshitsune Maeda, Edo period warlord (1594–1658)

After becoming the adopted heir of his elder brother, Toshitsune Maeda became the ruler of the Kaga Domain (in west-central Honshū), but he had one strange characteristic. He neglected to take care of his nose hairs. The long hairs that extended from his nose were often the subject of ridicule by those around him, and his retainers thought it was embarrassing. But Toshitsune had a reason for this. At that time, there was a tense relationship between the Tokugawa Shogunate and the outside daimyo (feudal lords). In order to suppress the rumors of rebellion propagated by the shogunate, Toshitsune allowed himself to be made fun of, which lowered his adversaries' defenses. It is said that Toshitsune's government established the city of Kanazawa and amassed great wealth from the salt mines in Noto, and for that his name is recorded in history.

It is important not to take yourself too seriously, and to have the courage to let yourself be made fun of.

"I have always observed that to succeed in the world one should seem a fool, but be wise."
—MONTESQUIEU, FRENCH POLITICAL PHILOSOPHER (1689–1755)

"Debase yourself and praise your enemy to lower his defenses."
—SUN TZU, CHINESE WARLORD (544-496 BC)

"If you are being kicked from behind, at least you are standing in front of someone."
—BILLY GRAHAM, AMERICAN PREACHER (1918–)

KEEP TALKING EVEN WHEN IGNORED.

Anne Sullivan, American educator (1866–1936)

Anne Sullivan was a private tutor who went to see a seven-year-old girl. The girl was uncontrollable, selfish, and never listened to what anyone said. Because of her disability, the girl was unable to speak, see, or hear, and it was extremely difficult for her to understand others. Although she felt many times that her heart would break, Anne continued trying to communicate with the girl. No matter how violent or resistant the girl became, Anne faced her with devotion. As a result, the girl—Helen Keller—grew into an amazing woman. She said, "Miss Sullivan showed me the light."

Even when someone doesn't act the way you want them to, persevere and continue speaking sincerely. This is how we build strong relationships.

QUOTES OF THE GREATS

"If we continue with kindness, even a man without a fragment of conscience will accept it."
—MARCUS AURELIUS, ROMAN EMPEROR (121–180)

"It seems natural that a strong camaraderie begins from doubt and opposition."
—ÉMILE-AUGUSTE CHARTIER (ALAIN), FRENCH PHILOSOPHER (1868–1951)

"If one does not understand a person, one tends to regard him as a fool."
—CARL GUSTAV JUNG, SWISS PSYCHIATRIST (1875–1961)

DON'T DEPEND ON THE RED STRING OF FATE.

Akio Morita, cofounder of Sony (1921–1999)

Akio Morita, cofounder of Sony, wanted to make his company into a global enterprise. The most urgent first step in advancing into the American market was to build personal connections with the business elite. But Morita couldn't just wait for these meetings to happen on their own. So in order to get to know the American business elite, he moved his family to the United States and held events almost daily at his house, to which he invited those he wanted to meet. People gathered at the parties until even the top journalists and biggest names in finance started attending. At the same time, Morita went to Broadway plays, polished his English, and mastered idiomatic expressions and jokes. In this way, Morita established broad personal connections in America and led Sony down the road to success.

Don't depend on the red string of fate. Forge your destiny for yourself.

QUOTES OF THE GREATS

"We make our own fortunes and we call them fate."

—BENJAMIN DISRAELI, BRITISH POLITICIAN (1804–1881)

"Men are free to determine their own destinies."

—KARL MARX, GERMAN PHILOSOPHER AND ECONOMIST (1818–1883)

"I shall seize fate by the throat; it will never bend me completely to its will."

—LUDWIG VAN BEETHOVEN, GERMAN COMPOSER (1770–1827)

59

MARRIAGE IS MOSTLY ABOUT LOOKING IN THE SAME GENERAL DIRECTION.

Anna Snitkina, second wife of Dostoyevsky and stenographer (1846–1918)

The Russian author Dostoyevsky loved gambling. Having squandered his assets on roulette, Dostoyevsky wrote *The Gambler* to make some much-needed money. The one who took down the dictations for this book was none other than his wife, Anna. When Dostoyevsky hit a wall in his writing, he would typically turn to gambling. Anna knew this and looked on in silence. Obliging Dostoyevsky's requests, Anna would draw from their household assets and let him gamble until he was content. At the same time, she also handled all the negotiations and complicated contracts with the publishers and made her husband focus on his writing. When he reflected on what his wife had done, Dostoyevsky found that he had lost the urge to gamble.

Even though we cannot change everything about our partners, if we are looking in the same direction, we will always find harmony.

QUOTES OF THE GREATS

"We must resemble each other a little in order to understand each other, but we must be a little different to love each other."
—PAUL GÉRALDY, FRENCH POET (1885–1983)

"Keep your eyes wide open before marriage, half shut afterward."
—BENJAMIN FRANKLIN, AMERICAN WRITER AND STATESMAN (1706–1790)

"Man and woman—they are so different and complex that even if they spend their lives together, in order to understand and love each other, it would not be enough."
—AUGUSTE COMTE, FRENCH SOCIOLOGIST (1798–1857)

60

A GOOD RELATIONSHIP CAN BE DEVELOPED WITH ANYONE.

Atsuko Saisho, Meiji period poet (1826–1900)

Atsuko Saisho served as a court lady to the empress and was a poet of the imperial court. However, when her husband died at age twenty-eight, Atsuko was forced to move to Kagoshima to take care of her mother-in-law. Her mother-in-law was very difficult to deal with and treated Atsuko cruelly. One day her mother-in-law sarcastically told her to recite a poem about the cruelty and nastiness of a belligerent old woman. Atsuko recited the following poem, which brought her mother-in-law to tears.

Not knowing the heart
of my mother-in-law, kinder
than that of the Buddha,
people seem to call her
a harridan, why I wonder—

Try to touch the hearts of even the most difficult people, and your feelings will speak to them.

QUOTES OF THE GREATS

"When you differ with a man, show him, by your looks, by your bearing, and by everything that you do or say, that you love him."
—PAUL DOUGLAS, AMERICAN POLITICIAN AND ECONOMIST (1892–1976)

"If we cannot end now our differences, at least we can help make the world safe for diversity."
—JOHN F. KENNEDY, THIRTY-FIFTH PRESIDENT OF THE UNITED STATES (1917–1963)

"The wisest man I have ever known once said to me: 'Nine out of every ten people improve on acquaintance,' and I have found his words true."
—FRANK SWINNERTON, ENGLISH AUTHOR (1884–1982)

HOPE

· · · · · · · · · · · · · · · ·

61

SEPARATION LEADS TO A NEW BEGINNING.

Nikola Tesla, Serbian electrical engineer and inventor (1856–1943)

The inventor Nikola Tesla, born in what is now Croatia, was the first person to use alternating electrical currents. After discovering the principles of alternating current, Tesla went to the United States to work for Thomas Edison, whom he admired. However, Edison's activities were devoted to direct current electricity, and he did not accept Tesla's ideas about alternating current. Edison had an unshakable faith in the superiority of direct current. After one year, Tesla quit and started his own company to research and develop alternating current electrical systems.

Even great thinkers have different aspirations and ways of thinking. If you must go on a different path, think of the separation in a positive light and strive forward.

"Change is tough. But it is hard to avoid in the business world. What you are left with is only a break from the past, though you may feel some reluctance to part ways."
—JACK WELCH, AMERICAN BUSINESSMAN (1935–)

"One doesn't discover new lands without consenting to lose sight, for a very long time, of the shore."
—ANDRÉ GIDE, FRENCH NOVELIST (1869–1951)

"There is no end. There is no beginning. There is only the infinite passion of life."
—FEDERICO FELLINI, ITALIAN FILM DIRECTOR (1920–1993)

QUOTES OF THE GREATS

Harrison Ford, American actor (1942–)

Harrison Ford went to Hollywood at age twenty-two to become an actor. But the only offers that came were for minor parts, and his big chance seemed like it would never come. It became difficult to support himself, so Ford took up work as a carpenter while he continued acting in small parts and keeping his eyes out for his big chance. Several years had passed when Ford got a great recommendation from someone in the film industry whose Beverly Hills home he worked on. A few small bit acting parts followed, but it wasn't until he was thirty-four that Ford finally got his break in *Star Wars* and became an "instant" star.

Don't give up, continue in earnest, and your reward will come.

QUOTES OF THE GREATS

"If we had no winter, the spring would not be so pleasant; if we did not sometimes taste of adversity, prosperity would not be so welcome."
—ANNE BRADSTREET (1612–1672)

"Everything changes for the better. Trust in that and patiently endure. After you have endured, you will obtain an unimaginable power."
—MAHATMA GANDHI, INDIAN LAWYER AND SOCIAL MOVEMENT LEADER (1869–1948)

"Destiny guides our fates more favorably than we could have expected."
—MIGUEL DE CERVANTES, SPANISH AUTHOR (1547–1616)

INSPIRATION COMES THROUGH DEEP REFLECTION

Leonardo da Vinci, Italian artist (1452–1519)

When Leonardo da Vinci was painting *The Last Supper*, he was unable to paint the face of Judas, who betrayed Jesus Christ, and could not finish the painting. The abbot of Santa Maria delle Grazie church was annoyed by this and demanded that da Vinci finish at once. Da Vinci thought to himself and realized that he had painted the faces and depictions of the other apostles from his own imagination. Perhaps the reason he couldn't paint Judas's face was because there was no one around him like Judas. But then he realized that there was in fact someone who could be the model for Judas. It was the abbot who had been in front of him the whole time. Using the abbot as a model, da Vinci was able to paint the face of Judas and complete *The Last Supper*.

Don't give up when you hit an obstacle. Keep thinking and an idea will come from where you least expect it.

QUOTES OF THE GREATS

"Only one who devotes himself to a cause with his whole strength and soul can be a true master. For this reason mastery demands all of a person."
—ALBERT EINSTEIN, GERMAN PHYSICIST (1879–1955)

"All inventions are knowledge born out of desperation. Ideas are the gifts given only to those who have suffered for them."
—SOICHIRO HONDA, FOUNDER OF HONDA (1906–1991)

"A discovery is said to be an accident meeting a prepared mind."
—ALBERT SZENT-GYÖRGYI, HUNGARIAN PHYSIOLOGIST (1893–1986)

Momofuku Ando, founder of Nissin Food Products Co. (1910–2007)

Momofuku Ando, founder of Nissin Food Products Company, was imprisoned on what he always maintained were false charges brought against him by the Allied Forces that occupied Japan after World War II. He experienced extreme hunger during his imprisonment, and understood that without food, people are incapable of doing anything. At age forty-six, Ando lost all his assets when the credit association he was running went bankrupt. He recalled his experience of hunger in prison as he started a new company, and decided to research nutrition. In a small shed that he built behind his house, Ando carried out his research and, through trial and error, invented the world's first instant ramen. As of 2011, Nissin Food Products has sold over 40 billion Cup Noodles in eighty countries around the world.

Use your experience of hardship to make something great. You will be amazed by what you end up with.

"If you've never eaten while crying, you don't know what life tastes like."
—JOHANN WOLFGANG VON GOETHE, GERMAN AUTHOR (1749–1832)

"Dreams are born from discontentment. People who are satisfied with their lives do not dream. There may be places where people dream—in squalid places, hospitals, and jail cells."
—HENRY DE MONTHERLANT, FRENCH AUTHOR (1895–1972)

"From suffering to delight."
—LUDWIG VAN BEETHOVEN, GERMAN COMPOSER (1770–1827)

GO TO A BRIGHTER PLACE.

Yukichi Fukuzawa, founder of Keio Gijuku (University) (1835–1901)

From when he was a child, Yukichi Fukuzawa rushed to do whatever captured his attention. When he wanted to try to make aqueous ammonia he did his own experiments in his backyard, which caused quite an alarm in his neighborhood because of the strong smell. After teaching himself to speak Dutch, he went to Yokohama to see if he could communicate with the foreigners there. But he quickly discovered that most of the foreigners there spoke English, not Dutch. So he quickly began studying English, and he was able to sail to America on the ship *Kanrin Maru*. He collected his experiences with Western culture in his book *Seiyo Jijo* (*Things Western*), and taught what he had learned overseas to the younger generation, producing a great number of excellent students.

Go out and explore this fascinating world. That is how you will grow into your best self.

QUOTES OF THE GREATS

"The world is filled with a light brighter than any can imagine."
—GILBERT K. CHESTERTON, ENGLISH AUTHOR (1874–1936)

"Man can learn nothing except by going from the known to the unknown."
—CLAUDE BERNARD, FRENCH PHYSIOLOGIST (1813–1878)

"The future has many names: For the weak, it means the unattainable. For the fearful, it means the unknown. For the courageous, it means opportunity."
—VICTOR HUGO, FRENCH POET (1802–1885)

Henry Ford, founder of the Ford Motor Company (1863–1947)

Henry Ford, the king of automobiles, wanted to make the automobile that he created while working as a technician into a business. But his first company was dissolved when the vehicles he produced were found to be of lower quality (and higher price) than Ford himself wanted. Ford left another company after disputes with investors and management. But Ford did not quit, and his next company—the Ford Motor Company—produced the Model T and sold over 15 million vehicles worldwide. On the way to success, Ford experienced bankruptcy multiple times. He is quoted as saying the following: "One who fears failure limits his activities. Failure is only the opportunity to more intelligently begin again."

We will meet countless hardships in our lives. But as long as we are alive, we can make a new start.

"Even if I fall down ninety-nine times, the hundredth time, too, I'll get up!"

—VINCENT VAN GOGH, DUTCH PAINTER (1853–1890)

"No matter how great your misfortunes, the greatest misfortune of all is to give in to despair."

—JEAN-HENRI FABRE, FRENCH ENTOMOLOGIST (1823–1915)

"The optimist sees the donut, the pessimist sees the hole."

—OSCAR WILDE, IRISH AUTHOR (1854–1900)

QUOTES OF THE GREATS

YOU'LL BE ALL RIGHT IF
YOU HAVE A PLACE TO SLEEP.

Walt Disney, founder of the Walt Disney Company (1901–1966)

People around the world know Disney as an entertainment giant, but Disney's journey to success was not always a smooth one. In 1941, faced with a severe labor strike, business at Disney Studios seemed like it would come to a halt. Walt Disney is reported to have addressed all of his employees: "I've lost my entire fortune twice during the last twenty years. The first time was in 1923 before I came to Hollywood. I was completely out of money and didn't have anything to eat for three days, and I slept on top of some tattered cloths in a dirty studio. The second time was in 1928. My brother Roy and I mortgaged our entire fortune for this studio. It was not a great sum of money, but it was all that we had." In this way, Walt talked honestly with the workers and was able to end the strike.

In order to accomplish great things, we sometimes have to endure hard circumstances. But as long as we have a dream and a place to sleep, we can overcome many obstacles.

"He who knows he has enough is rich."

—LAOZI, CHINESE PHILOSOPHER (6TH CENTURY BC)

"Persuade thyself that imperfection and inconvenience are the natural lot of mortals, and there will be no room for discontent, neither for despair."

—TOKUGAWA IEYASU, SHOGUN AND FEUDAL LORD (1543–1616)

"Living is simple; dreaming is hard."

—RALPH WALDO EMERSON, AMERICAN ESSAYIST (1803–1882)

Ray Kroc, owner of McDonald's (1902–1984)

Ray Kroc bought the franchise rights to McDonald's from the McDonald brothers and embarked on the McDonald's business at age fifty-two. Until that point, he had been overworking himself as a salesman selling blenders and mixers, and his health was poor. But he worked through his difficulties. He strived toward his future goals, going to every McDonald's store across the country, walking around each store on his pain-stricken legs, observing every detail of how the franchises were run, never compromising, and led McDonald's down the path to becoming a global enterprise. Kroc is quoted as saying, "As long as you're green, you're growing. As soon as you're ripe, you start to rot."

Life is only what you make it. At some point—at any moment—the path will open to you.

QUOTES OF THE GREATS

"It is never too late to make up your mind."
—STANLEY BALDWIN, BRITISH POLITICIAN (1867–1947)

"When people ask me why I don't retire, this is what I tell them: 'I'd rather work myself to dust than just sit there collecting rust.' "
—COLONEL SANDERS, FOUNDER OF KENTUCKY FRIED CHICKEN (1890–1980)

"It takes the whole of life to learn how to live."
—LUCIUS ANNAEUS SENECA, ROMAN PHILOSOPHER (C. 4 **BC–AD** 65)

BIBLIOGRAPHY

- Auletta, Ken. *Googled: The End of the World As We Know It*. New York: Penguin, 2009.
- Brandt, Richard L. *One Click: Jeff Bezos and the Rise of Amazon.com*. New York: Portfolio, 2011.
- Calonius, Erik. *Ten Steps Ahead: What Separates Successful Business Visionaries from the Rest of Us*. New York: Portfolio, 2011.
- Carlin, John. *Invictus: Nelson Mandela and the Game That Made a Nation*. New York: Penguin, 2009.
- Carnegie, Dale. *Dale Carnegie's Scrapbook: A Treasury of the Wisdom of the Ages*. Ed. Dorothy Carnegie. Np: Snowball Publishing, 2013.
- Ford, Henry. *My Life & Work: An Autobiography of Henry Ford*. Sioux Falls, South Dakota: Greenbook Publications, 2010.
- Gostick, Adrian and Chester Elton. *All In: How the Best Managers Create a Culture of Belief and Drive Big Results*. New York: Free Press, 2012.
- Guiles, Fred Lawrence. *Legend: The Life and Death of Marilyn Monroe*. New York: Stein & Day, 1984.
- Isaacson, Walter. *Steve Jobs*. New York: Simon & Schuster, 2011.

- "Ryokoki sakka Mark Twain: Shirarezaru tabi to toki no hibi," by Eichi Iizuka, Sairyusha.
- Mandela, Nelson. *Long Walk to Freedom: The Autobiography of Nelson Mandela*. New York: Holt, Rinehart and Winston, 2000.
- Tanase, Virgil. *Tchekhov*. Paris: Gallimard Education, 2008.
- "Hakubutsugaku no kyojin Henri Fabre," by Daizaburo Okumoto, Shueisha.
- *How was Helen Keller taught? Anne Sullivan's Records* by Anne Sullivan.
- "Monozukuri tamashi: Kono genten wo wasureta kiggyo wa horobiru," by Dai Ibuka, Yoshiro Yanagishita Ed, Sunmark Publishing.
- "Nippon Kinshu-undo no 80-nen," by Kanji Oshio, Japanese Temperance Union.
- "Retsujo den: Densetsu ni natta onnatachi," by Eitsuko Makisumi, Meiji Shoin KK.
- "Stories of men who won success over age 40," by Mitsuhiro Sato, Alphapolis.
- "The BEST of SUCCESS Magazine," Scott DeGarmo (Ed.), translated by Richard H. Morita, frontier-books.
- Singh, Dr. Simon. *Fermat's Last Theorem: The Story of a Riddle That Confounded the World's Greatest Minds for 358 Years*. Glasgow, UK: 4th Estate, 2002.
- "Otona no tame no izinden," by Takeichi Kihara, Shinchosha.
- "Kokoro wo sodateru hajimete no denki 101 nin," Kodansha.
- "Denki jinbutsu jiten sekai-hen," Toshio Nishiyama (Ed.), Hoikusha.
- "Kokoeo ni shimiru tensai no itsuwa 20," by Daiki Yamada, Kodansha.

- "Hito wo ugokasu [Meigen, Itsuwa] taishusei," by Kenji Yamada, Hideo Shinozawa (Ed.), Kodansha.
- "Hito wo ugokasu ichinichi hitowa katuyo-jiten," Kodansha.
- *Sekai jinbutsu itsuwa daijiten,* by Haruhiko Asakura, Ichiro Miura (Ed.), Kadokawa.
- "Shukan gendai," 2011.11.5.
- "Shukan shincho," 2012.10.4.
- "Gekkan BOSS," 2008.7.
- "Nikkei entertainment," 2003.9.20.
- "Sekai meigen kakugen," Mollis Maloux (Ed.), translated by Tomo Shimazu, Tokyodo shuppan.
- "Sekai meigen dai-jiten," by Ken Kajiyama, Meijishoin.
- "Sekai meigen zensho dai 1 kan," Yoshizo Kawamori Ed, Tokyo-sogensha.
- "Sekai meigen zensho dai 2 kan," Yoshizo Kawamori Ed, Tokyo-sogensha.
- "Sekai meigen zensho dai 5 kan," Yoshizo Kawamori Ed, Tokyo-sogensha.
- "Meigen meiku ni tsuyokunaru," Sekaibunkasha.
- "Aizoban zayu no mei, zayu no mei" Kenkyu-kai (Ed.), Metropolitan Press.
- "Mei monku koroshi monku," by Takahiko Ifukube, Chobun-sha.
- "For Leaders," by Wes Roberts, Hideki Wada (Ed.), translated by Keiko Watarai, Shodensha.
- "Ogon no kotoba," by Katsuichiro Kamei, Daiwashobo
- "Ongakuka no meigen," by Nobu Hiyama, Yamaha Music Media.
- "Jinsei ni kansuru 439 no meigen," by Shiro Kannabe, Futabasha.
- "Jinsei no shishin ga mitsukaru zayu no mei 1300," Takarajimasha.

- "Edison no kotoba," Kazuyuki Hamada, Daiwashobo.
- "Girishia Roma meigen-shu," by Shigetake Yagenuma, Iwanami shoten.
- Woods, Earl. *Training a Tiger: A Father's Guide to Raising a Winner in Both Golf and Life.* New York: HarperCollins, 1997.

WEBSITES

Meigen-Navi: http://www.meigennavi.net/
Meigen-DB: http://systemincome.com/
Web Monument Quote Collection: http://sekihi.net/
Famous Quotes You'll Want to Make into your Motto:
  http://za-yu.com/

PHOTO CREDITS

Numbering corresponds to chapter numbers.

1. © AlenaOzerova
2. ondagoarts ©123RF
3. © vamapaull/iStock
4. Akimasa Harada/Getty Images
5. © nickpo/iStock
6. andreykuzmin ©123RF
7. goodween123 ©123RF
8. amikos ©123RF
9. vdovin_vn/Shutterstock
10. 5464316719/Shutterstock
11. Jeffrey Sylvester/Getty Images
12. LCLPhoto/iStock
13. funix ©123RF
14. andreshka ©123RF
15. Martin Ruegner/Getty Images
16. © Tomwang112/iStock
17. ecobo©123RF
18. Richard Pearson/Getty Images
19. Akimasa Harada/Getty Images
20. sbworld8©123RF
21. Aptypkok©123RF
22. Joshua Sterrett Photography/Getty Images

23. © Ira Bachinskaya/iStock
24. mirlex ©123RF
25. schubbel/Shutterstock
26. Serg_v ©123RF
27. evdoha ©123RF
28. © AlenaMozhjer /iStock
29. GK Hart/Vikki Hart/Getty Images
30. anyka ©123RF
31. Tancrediphoto.com
32. © 101cats/iStock
33. © Elena Trash
34. efenzi/Getty Images
35. Tony Campbell/Shutterstock
36. Dragan Todorovic/Getty Images
37. Hadfields/Getty Images
38. kitigan ©123RF
39. aleksandr foto/Shutterstock
40. idmanjoe ©123RF
41. websubstance ©123RF
42. natulrich ©123RF
43. Mayte Torres/Getty Images
44. Dennis Guyitt
45. © ewastudio/iStock
46. bibikoff/Getty Images
47. kertis ©123RF
48. © spxChrome/iStock
49. © Ira Bachinskaya/iStock
50. Stringer/Corbis
51. © MKucova/iStock
52 . Ysbrand Cosijn/Shutterstock
53. Ary6/Getty Images
54. miolana ©123RF

55. Sanna Pudas/Getty
56. karamysh/Shutterstock
57. Shinya Sasaki/Aflo
58. fieldsphotos ©123RF
59. Meredith Parmelee/Getty Images
60. mashe©123RF
61. Rita Kochmarjova/Shutterstock
62. vvvita/Shutterstock
63. © Jorge Pereira/iStock
64. Michelle Kelley Photography/Getty Images
65. korionov ©123RF
66. roadbully ©123RF
67. Liliya Kulianionak/Shutterstock
68. FotoYakov/Shutterstock

ABOUT THE AUTHORS

Keiya Mizuno is one of Japan's bestselling authors today. His most successful books include *The Guru Elephant's Guide to Achieving the Dream Life* (over 2 million copies sold; *Yume Wo Kanaeru Zou* in Japanese) and the Life Lessons animal book series (over 1.9 million copies sold; Jinsei Wa . . . series in Japanese). Keiya graduated from Keio University with a degree in economics.

   Official blog: *Ukeru Nikki* http://ameblo.jp/mizunokeiya/
   Twitter @mizunokeiya

Naoki Naganuma is a budding author who has coauthored two books with Keiya, including *Life Works Itself Out*. Naoki graduated from Nihon University, Faculty of Arts, where he studied advertising and documentary filmmaking.

   Official blog: *n_naganuma no nikki* http://d.hatena.ne.jp/n_
     naganuma/
   Twitter @n_naganuma